Lorna Robinson

TELLING tales in GREEK

Illustrated by Soham De

For my dear little Rachel, who loves the tales of Odysseus

- LR

Contents

Acknowledgements

I would like to thank Evelien Bracke and Sebastian Hyams, both of whom provided very helpful feedback on drafts of this book. I would also like to thank my Greek group at Cheney School, who inspired me to write this, and provided much inspiration.

I am very grateful to dear friends and family who listened to me talking about this, looked at drafts, and provided love and support – and most especially to Duncan, without whom, I would be lost. – LR

I would like to thank my parents for their support and love. To Prachi for her assistance, contribution and keeping me company during late hours at work. – SD

χαιρε

Welcome to this book of tales. My name is Odysseus and I come from Ithaca, a rugged island which has mountains with quivering leaves, and which nurtures fine, strong men. Yet I've spent much of my life far away from the beloved shores of my homeland.

I've been called many names – wily, cunning, the man of many strategies, a teller of tales. In this book, I will tell you the story of my travels.

You will discover how I came to be so far from home, and some of the fantastical and often frightening things we met along the way!

While doing this, I would like to introduce you to my language, Ancient Greek, as I tell my tales.

Before we begin, I will introduce you to the letters. Here is what they look like – and what they sound like. The first thing you might like to do is practice writing the letters, and then try to write your own name.

Mine is Ὀδυσσευς.

Lower case	Capital	Name of letter	Sound of letter
α	A	alpha	a
β	B	beta	b
γ	Γ	gamma	g (as in 'get')
δ	Δ	delta	d
ε	E	epsilon	e (as in 'get')
ζ	Z	zeta	z
η	H	eta	long e (like in 'obey')
θ	Θ	theta	th
ι	I	iota	i
κ	K	kappa	k
λ	Λ	lambda	l
μ	M	mu	m
ν	N	nu	n
ξ	Ξ	xi	x (as in 'fox')
ο	O	omicron	short o (as in 'hot')
π	Π	pi	p
ρ	P	rho	r
σ ς when at end of a word	Σ	sigma	s
τ	T	tau	t
υ	Y	upsilon	u, y
φ	Φ	phi	f
χ	X	chi	ch (as in choir)
ψ	Ψ	psi	ps
ω	Ω	omega	long o (as in 'vote')

You'll notice that some letters in English just don't exist, so try to get as close as you can with the letters below. If your name begins with an H, we would write this by putting something called a rough 'breathing' in front of the first letter – have a look at this example:

	smooth	**rough**
	ἐν	ἑν
pronunciation	en	hen

Here are some of the characters you will meet in this book – can you work out who they are?

Ἀθηνη
Ἀχιλλευς
Ζευς
Πολυφημος
Ποσειδων
Ἀγαμεμνων
Κιρκη
Πατροκλος

Now that you've had a practice, I think we're ready to begin on our journey. By the way, did you work out what the title of this little chapter means?

chapter 1
The Golden Apple

All my travels and trials began with a competition at a wedding. Legend has it that long, long ago, a man, ὁ Πελευς, was sailing on the sea in a ship called the Argo (that's another story!), and he happened to glimpse in the gleaming sea water a goddess called ἡ θετις. They fell in love with each other, and ὁ Ζευς allowed that they should marry each other, a mortal and an immortal.

The king of the gods himself laid on the most lavish celebration of the wedding and all οἱ θεοι were invited – all except ἡ θεα of strife ἡ Ερις. It was felt she might cause trouble if she were there.

When she realised she had not been invited to this fabulous event, she was very unhappy. She decided to turn up with a χρυσεον μηλον which she had taken from the garden of αἱ Ἑσπεριδες.

το μηλον was inscribed with the words "καλλιστη" as a prize for the most beautiful goddess at the wedding.

Are you following so far? I've started to sprinkle Greek words here and there for you to get used to reading them. Below you can find out what they mean!

ὁ Πελευς = Peleus
ἡ Θετις = Thetis
ὁ Ζευς = Zeus
ἡ Ἐρις = Eris
οἱ θεοι = the gods
ἡ θεα = the goddess
χρυσεον μηλον = a golden apple
αἱ Ἑσπεριδες = the Hesperides, nymphs of the evening
το μηλον = the apple
καλλιστη = for the most beautiful

Have you noticed how names have ὁ or ἡ in front of them (remember that the breathing I mentioned earlier means you pronounce them "ho" and "he")? These are both words for "the" – the word for "the" changes according to the noun it is with – but in ancient Greek, it also appears in front of names. You don't need to say "the Peleus", for example! Just ignore it – you'll get used to it being there.

There is also a word for the, "το", which you may have noticed went before "μηλον". This is the word for the which Greek uses for nouns which are "neuter". We'll see more of those in later chapters.

Let's carry on with the story

αἱ θεαι, ἡ Ἡρα, ἡ Ἀθηνη και ἡ Ἀφροδιτη, all claimed the prize should be theirs, so ὁ Ζευς decided to ask a Trojan prince, called ὁ Παρις, to judge the competition. αἱ θεαι each offered him an ἀθλον to encourage him to choose her. ἡ Ἡρα offered ὁ Παρις command over all of Asia and Europe! ἡ Ἀθηνη offered him σοφια and skill in war. Finally, ἡ Ἀφροδιτη said that she would give him the most beautiful γυνη in the world, ἡ Ἑλενη of Sparta, wife of the mighty and powerful king ὁ Μενελαυς.

command all over Asia and Europe

σοφια and skill in war

most beautiful γυνη in the world

So which goddess do you think Paris chose? Perhaps you already know the story. Here are some of the names and words you met in the passage:

αἱ θεαι = the goddesses
ἡ Ἥρα = Hera, wife of Zeus
ἡ Ἀθηνη = Athene, goddess of war and wisdom
ἡ Ἀφροδιτη = Aphrodite, goddess of love
και = and
ὁ Παρις = Paris, a Trojan prince
ἀθλον = a prize
σοφια = wisdom
γυνη = a woman
ἡ Ἑλενη = Helen, wife of the king of Sparta
ὁ Μενελαυς = king of Sparta

ὁ Παρις chose ἡ Ἑλενη and that was the beginning of my twenty years of troubles and travel.

Further Tales

The wedding of Peleus and Thetis was supposed to have been the most lavish of all celebrations! Another tale-teller, who lived many centuries later than me, Catullus, described the dazzling spread and gleaming cups and plates all through a sprawling and elegant palace.

Can you draw a picture of this feast? What might have been eaten and drunk? What did the plates and cups look like?

The Hesperides were the nymphs of the evening, who tended to a beautiful garden in the farthest western corner of the world. There a tree with golden apples grew; if someone ate an apple, it gave them immortality. As well as looking after the garden, the nymphs occasionally ate the apples.

Hera, wife of Zeus, did not trust the nymphs, so she placed a hundred-headed dragon there to guard the tree.

No one is quite sure how many Hesperides there were – here are some of their names. Can you transliterate them?

ἡ Αἴγλη   ἡ Ὑγιεια
ἡ Ἀρεθουσα   ἡ Ἑσπερια
ἡ Χρυσοθεμις

There is some uncertainty about whether the fruit from the tree were apples. It was thought that what were thought of by the Greeks as golden apples may actually have been oranges!

As you might imagine, when the Trojan prince Paris stole Helen away, the mighty King Menelaus was very angry. Paris arrived back in Troy and everyone there was dismayed and frightened.

His brother Hector and father, King Priam, knew what this would mean: war. And not just any war, but the greatest war we had ever seen, a war that would be talked about for centuries and more.

It might seem ridiculous that all this happened as a result of an apple! Helen's beauty was legendary, even in our own time, and so perhaps Paris felt that he had no choice.

Here are some simple Greek sentences which explain the next part of the story. There are words and new grammar to help you. For now, have a go at reading them aloud, and see if you can guess at any of the new words.

ὁ Παρις ἀγει την Ἑλενην προς την πολιν.

ὁ Μενελαυς και ὁ Ἀγαμεμνων ἀγουσι χιλιας ναυς.

μακρος στρατος βαινει προς την πολιν.

Words

ἀγει = leads πολις = city μακρος = large
ἀγουσι = lead ναυς = ships στρατος = army
προς = towards χιλιας = a thousand βαινει = goes

There are two things to notice with these sentences.

The first is about the verbs, In sentence one and three the verbs both end in -ει, but in the second sentence, the verb ends in -ουσι.

Why might that be?

It's to do with singular and plural subjects.

The subject is what's doing the action, and in sentence one and three, it is a singular subject – *Paris leads* and *an army goes*.

In the second sentence it is plural – *Paris and Menelaus are leading the ships.*

In Greek, a verb has a stem – a bit at the start which doesn't change – and then endings which change according to who is doing the action. See below for how it works:

stem + ending

ἀγ-ει = he/she/it leads
ἀγ-ουσι = they lead

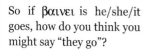

So if βαινει is he/she/it goes, how do you think you might say "they go"?

Among those many ships from all across Greece, I sailed with my ships of men from my island of Ithaca. I bade farewell to Penelope, my loyal wife, and Telemachus, my baby son, and we set off towards glory in battle, none of us knowing if we would return...

Many different lands sent ships of men to fight in the Trojan War.

ἡ Βοιωτια πεμπει πεντηκοντα ναυς.
αἱ Ἀθηναι πεμπουσι πεντηκοντα ναυς.
αἱ Μυκηναι πεμπουσι ἑκατον ναυς.
ἡ Σπαρτη πεμπει ἑξηκοντα ναυς.
ἡ Κρητη πεμπει ὀγδοηκοντα ναυς.
ἡ Ἰθακη πεμπει δυοκαιδεκα ναυς.

There were many other places which also sent ships – in total, it was more than a thousand ships that set off for that war over beautiful Helen.

Words

πεμπει = he/she/it sends
πεμπουσι = they send
δυοκαιδεκα = twelve
πεντηκοντα = fifty
ἑξηκοντα = sixty
ὀγδοηκοντα = eighty
ἑκατον = one hundred

Have you worked out the names of the various places which sent ships? Here is a map showing all the places I have mentioned – can you see where my own dear island, Ithaca, is?

There were many other places which sent ships to the beaches of Troy.

You can find them in book two of the Iliad – perhaps you can find a translation, and look up some of the other places.

If you draw yourself a map, you can draw these ships and places onto the map. How many ships did these other places send?

Numbers are one way in which my language has very clearly shaped English. Below are the Greek numbers from one to ten –have a go at transliterating them first. Can you come up with words in English that have come from these Greek words for numbers?

εἱς μια ἑν   τεσσαρες   ἑπτα
δυο   πεντε   ὀκτω
τρεις   ἑξ   ἑννεα
                                        δεκα

Can you imagine these ships from all over Greece gliding through the dark, glistening sea towards Troy?

What a sight it must have been for the gods.

I can still remember the creaking of the timber and the shouts of the sailors, and the feeling of excitement and dread in my heart...

chapter 3
The Quarrel on the Beach

Once all those dark ships had glided across the sparkling sea, they arrived at the beaches of the city of Troy, and that was when the fighting began. For ten long years we fought outside those high walls.

The Trojans had Hector, slayer of men, a brave and mighty warrior indeed. We had the godlike Achilles, a man who was born to kill.

The trouble was that Achilles had a strong temper, and disliked the leader of the Greek army, Agamemnon.

One day they had a quarrel that changed everything. The quarrel started over two girls whom Achilles and Agamemnon had taken as slaves in a raid on another Trojan city.

ἡ Βρισηις ἐστι κορη.

ὁ Ἀχιλλευς ἐχει την κορην Βρισηιν.

ἡ Χρισηις ἐστι κορη.

ὁ Ἀγαμεμνων ἐχει την κορην Χρισηιν.

Chryseis, the slave girl Agamemnon had taken, happened to be the daughter of a priest of the god Apollo.

He asked for his daughter to be returned, but Agamemnon was a stubborn and proud man. He refused. Her father then prayed to Apollo for help, and the god answered the prayer of his loyal priest.

ὁ Ἀπολλων πεμπει νοσον. ἡ νοσος ἐστι δεινη. πολλοι ἀνθρωποι ἀποθνησηκουσιν.

Words
κορη = girl
νοσος = disease
δεινη = terrible/strange
πολλοι = many
ἀποθνησκουσιν = die

Have you noticed how the word for disease – νοσος – changes its ending in the sentence. Why do you think it does that? I expect you may have guessed that when something or someone is the subject, it has one ending, but when it's the object it has another. Have a look at these endings:

	group one (mostly feminine)	group two (mostly masculine)	group two (neuter)
Subject	κορη θεα	φιλος (friend)	φυτον
Object	κορην θεαν	φιλον	φυτον

The object endings either add an "ν" or change an "ς" to an "ν". The exceptions to this are "neuter" nouns like φυτον meaning 'a plant', where the ending, "ν", stays the same for subject and object. "Neuter" means that the noun is neither masculine or feminine. In my language, all nouns are assigned a "gender".

The plague destroyed many of us, and we became desperate. We asked a seer to tell us what we should do to make it end. Of course, the answer was to return the girl Chryseis to her father.

Agamemnon was fiercely angry, and initially refused, but Achilles argued with him. It was a strange scene, there on the sandy beach, watching these two great men shouting at each other.

ὁ Ἀγαμεμνων λαμβανει την κορην Βρισηιν.
ὁ Ἀχιλλευς ἐχει μεγιστην ὀργην.

μεγιστην = very great   ὀργη = anger

Achilles glared darkly at the kingly Agamemnon, his eyes filled with a deep wrath. His τιμη (our word for the 'honour' a hero lives and dies for) had been insulted, and his proud warrior heart was not able to bear it.

Achilles stormed off and sat next to his tent on the windy beach, looking out at the bluegreen sea. As the waves crashed in before turning to running rivulets that danced forward then fled back, he sat and he watched and he turned over his immense anger in his heart.

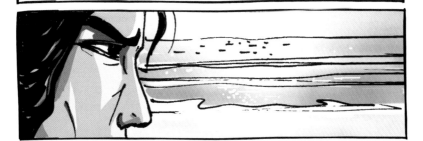

We gradually came to realise that we had lost mighty Achilles from the war, and we needed him desperately.

The word τιμη behaves rather like the word κορη – these words belong to the first group. Words like φιλος belong to the second group.

Translate the following sentence into Greek (and try not to peek at the answer below!):

How did that go? Here is what it should look like:
ὁ Ἀχιλλευς ἐχει την τιμην.

You might find it surprising that Greek uses the word 'the' in front of 'honour'. This is because we use the word 'the' when we are talking about concepts like honour, wisdom and friendship.

These are all things that aren't physical things, but exist as ideas in our minds. We Greeks were very interested in ideas and we spent a lot of time talking about them, but more on that another time.

Further Thoughts

Homer, the author of these stories, wrote down in detail the argument between Agamemnon and Achilles. He told us some of what they said to one another that dreadful day on the beach.

Can you write down what you think they might have said?

People have always been fascinated by the idea of the godlike hero Achilles sitting miserably on the sand away from the fighting, lost in his own feelings and thoughts. If you enjoy drawing, perhaps you could draw a picture of him on the beach of Troy, staring out at the sea...

Apollo, the archer god, brought the plague upon us Greeks. Apollo was known for many things other than archery – can you find out and list them? You might be surprised at how many roles he had!

Here are some of Greek names for things which were sacred to Apollo. Have a go at transliterating them, and then working out what they might mean? (you'll find the answers in the vocabulary in the back!)

λυρα   ὀμφαλος   δελφις   τοξον

See you in the next chapter!

Achilles sat on that beach for a very long time watching the sea roll in and out, and while he sat watching, we Greeks struggled against the mighty Trojans.

Their prince, Hector, was a very fine fighter, and we had no one to match him. I was sent to try and persuade him to return to the battlefield, but not even my wily words could change his heart! It took something that none of us were expecting to get Achilles back to fighting.

Can you translate these sentences which explain a bit more of the story?

ὁ Ἀχιλλευς ἐχει φιλον. ὁ φιλος ἐστι Πατροκλος.
ὁ Πατροκλος ἐχει ὀργην διοτι ὁ Ἀχιλλευς μενει ἐν τῃ
κυματωγῃ. ὁ Πατροκλος λαμβανει τα ὁπλα και ἀγει
τους ἀνθρωπους εἰς την μαχην.

Words
διοτι = because
εἰς = into/onto
ἐν = in/on
κυματωγη, ἡ = seashore
λαμβανει = takes
μαχη, ἡ = battle
μενει = stays
ὀργη, ἡ = anger
ὁπλα, τα = weapons
φιλος, ὁ = friend

The word "κυματωγη" actually means "where the waves break", which is of course the seashore! It's a rather beautiful word, I think.

You may notice a new ending on a word you have met before – ἀνθρωπους. This is the word for "men" when "men" is the object of the sentence. Here are the plural endings for group one and two nouns.

Singular:	group one	group two	group two neuter
Subject	μαχη	φιλος	φυτον
Object	μαχην	φιλον	φυτον

Plural:			
Subject	μαχαι	φιλοι	φυτα
Object	μαχας	φιλους	φυτα

You will notice how the plural subject and object endings for neuter nouns also stay the same, just like the singular endings you met in the last chapter.

33

Patroclus didn't take his own armour, though. He decided to take the armour of Achilles...

As he ran towards the walls of Troy, looking for all the world like Achilles, and the Greeks cheered joyfully! For the first time in many weeks, our army felt hopeful again. At last, there was a chance we might win this war.

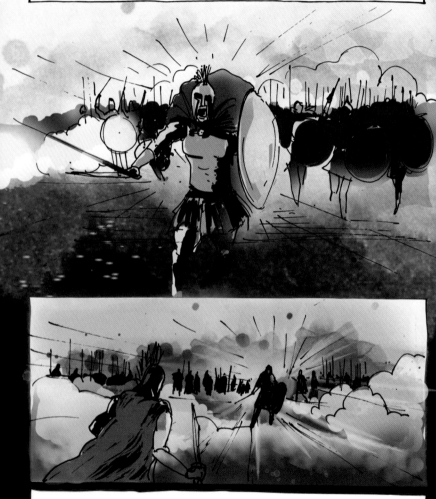

The man we all thought was Achilles himself fought bravely and killed many Trojans. Then he came face to face with Hector.

Everyone watched as they stood before one another, wondering what would happen next. Patroclus fought as well as he could, but he was no match for Hector who killed him easily. We were stunned into silence. Could Achilles really have been defeated by Hector, prince of Troy?

Hector himself could scarcely believe it, and he knelt down to remove the helmet from his victim.

A gasp rippled through the crowd. Patroclus lay dead on the floor, Achilles' dear friend. Everyone now knew that something dreadful would happen. Hector returned inside the walls of Troy, and waited, spending some precious moments with his wife and baby son.

Can you translate these sentences to discover the next part of the story?

ὁ Ἀχιλλευς βαινει προς την πυλην. ἐθελει ἀποκτεινειν τον Ἑκτορα.
ὁ Ἀχιλλευς μενει. ὁ δημος μενει. οἱ θεοι μενουσιν.
τελος ὁ Ἑκτωρ ἐκβαινει.

Words

ἀποκτεινειν = to kill   πυλη, ἡ = gate
ἐθελει = wants   τελος = finally
δημος, ὁ = the people   ὁ Ἑκτωρ = Hector (here as the subject)
προς = towards   τον Ἑκτορα = Hector (here as the object)

There Hector stood in front of the walls of his mighty city, while his
father and mother stretched their arms through the gates and begged
for him to come inside. Achilles stepped closer.

Suddenly, Hector felt his knees buckle, and, faced with this godlike warrior, and the thought of his death, he ran! He ran around the proud, high walls of his city and Achilles ran after him, as everyone looked on. Three times they ran around those walls. They ran past the springs where women used to wash their clothes in times of peace.

Hector finally found the strength to stop and face Achilles. He spoke to him:

"Let us at least make a pact that whoever wins will give the body of the loser to his people to bury with honour."

Achilles gave him a fierce, dark look. "There are no pacts between lions and men", he said.

The pair fought and everyone watched, as their weapons and armour gleamed in the sun, and the shrill clanks of sword against sword rang out.

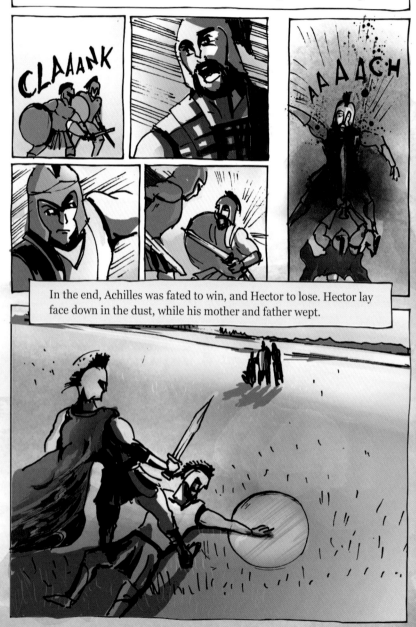

In the end, Achilles was fated to win, and Hector to lose. Hector lay face down in the dust, while his mother and father wept.

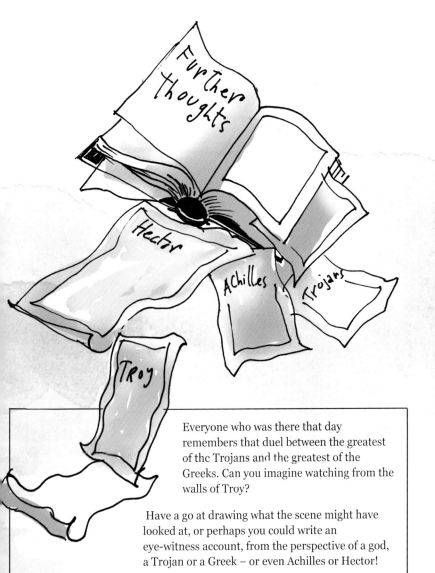

Everyone who was there that day remembers that duel between the greatest of the Trojans and the greatest of the Greeks. Can you imagine watching from the walls of Troy?

Have a go at drawing what the scene might have looked at, or perhaps you could write an eye-witness account, from the perspective of a god, a Trojan or a Greek – or even Achilles or Hector!

There are many who thought that it was the defeat of Hector which led to the Trojans losing the war. Of course, there is another story, which I will tell you about in the next chapter. It's fun to explore what might have happened in Hector hadn't been killed. Why don't you write an alternative version of the duel between Achilles and Hector – one where Hector isn't killed. What effect might that have on the outcome of the War?

chapter 5
The Wooden Horse

With Hector gone, the war continued, and both sides fought fiercely, but there was no respite. Day after day, we lost good men on either side and it seemed that the sound of clashing arms would go on forever.

At night, the fires of our Greek camps twinkled like the sparkles on the dark sea, and we thought of our homes. I thought of my wife Penelope and my son Telemachus. I had not seen them for ten long years.

It was in an evening like this that a plan appeared in my mind, and began to take shape...

δουρειος ἱππος

I suggested the idea to Agamemnon. Can you translate what I said to him?

λεγω "οί Τροιανοι λαμβανουσι τον ἱππον εἰς την Τροιαν.
ἀλλα ἀνθρωποι εἰσι ἐν τῳ ἱππῳ.
ἀνθρωποι ἀποκτεινουσι παντας τους πολεμιους."

ὁ Ἀγαμεμνων λεγει "ὦ Ὀδυσσευ, εἰ πολυμητις."

Words

ἀλλα = but
ἀποκτεινουσι = kill
δουρειος = wooden
εἰ = you are
ἐν τῳ ἱππῳ = in the horse
ἱππος = horse
λαμβανουσι = take
λεγω = I say
δουρειος = wooden
παντας τους πολεμιους = all the enemy
πολυμητις = wily, clever
ὦ Ὀδυσσευ = o Odysseus

Can you pick out all the verbs in the passage and write them down? What do you notice about the endings? So far, you've met the ending for "he/she/it" and the ending for "they", e.g.:

λαμβανει = he/she/it takes
λαμβανουσι = they take

There is a new ending here, though.
Did you notice "λεγω" - what did it mean?

I'm going to introduce you to all the endings in the present tense. Have a look below:

λαμβανω = I take
λαμβανεις = you (singular) take
λαμβανει = he/she/it takes
λαμβανομεν = we take
λαμβανετε = you (plural) take
λαμβανουσι(ν) = they take

Keep a look out for some of these new endings in the later passages and chapters!

And so the plan was set in place. The first task was to construct the great wooden creature. We chopped some timber from one of our ships, and using rope, we hauled the wood into place, making sure to make a large hollow belly for some of our men to hide inside.

Our fleet then sailed around the shore, and waited in hiding, pretending that we had surrendered and sailed away. They left the giant wooden horse standing on the beach, like a peace offering, but with our men inside.

The next morning, the Trojans found it standing there, and debated amongst themselves about what to do. Two Trojans, Sinon and Lycaon, stood up to speak.

"ἐστι δωρον" λεγει ὁ Σινων.
"ἐστι δολος" λεγει ὁ Λαοκοων.

Words

δολος, ὁ = trick
δωρον, το = gift

After much arguing on the beach, the Trojans make a decision that they came to deeply regret. They wheeled that mighty wooden horse right through the gates of their proud city, and through the streets, full of triumph, since they thought they had won and we were defeated.

I was one of the men inside that creature. It was cramped and dark, and the sound of cheering and the rumbling on the wheels filled our ears. At first we were terrified we would be discovered, but after a while, we just wanted to get out. Later that night, while the city slept after hearty celebrations, we were ready to move.

βαινομεν ἐκ του ἱππου, και τρεχομεν δια των ὁδων. ἀποκτεινομεν τους ἀνθρωπους λαμβανομεν τας γυναικας. νυν αἱ γυναικες εἰσι δουλοι.

Words

δια των ὁδων = through the roads   αἱ γυναικες, τας γυναικας = the women
δουλος, ὁ = a slave   νυν = now
ἐκ του ἱππου = out of the horse   τρεχω = I run

Troy fell that same night. Its people were either killed or captured. It was all down to my trickery. As it happens, not every man was destroyed. A certain Trojan called Aeneas escaped, carrying his aged father on his back, and he went on a very long journey, and finally founded a mighty empire. But that's another story for another time. In the next few chapters you'll hear a few stories from my own long journey to get home.

Further Thoughts

Building that wooden horse on the beach was no easy task – we had to use what we had and we worked hard! I still remember the beads of sweat pouring down my face as I roped great frames of timber in place, excited at my plan, but fearing what might happen if it went wrong. How would you construct your own wooden horse? One easy way to do this is with the following:

two corks
five cocktail sticks
two pins

Be careful not to prick your fingers with these! Can you work out how to make a little model horse? Of course, there are plenty of other ways to do it too. I think my wooden horse was rather a clever trick, and it certainly worked. Can you devise a similar trick – how might you have found a way to take the city of Troy?

chapter 6
The Lotus Eaters

So the war was over and we had won, thanks to my wooden horse. The Greek ships began their journeys home, and I began mine.

My head was full of Ithaca, the beautiful, rugged island where my wife and son were waiting for me. We set sail westwards towards home, the ships gliding through the dark sea, and the sunshine gleaming on the waves. I was excited to be on my way home, as were all my men. We could almost taste the air of Ithaca on our lips as we sailed.

Unfortunately, though, it did not work out so simply for us.
Read on in Greek to hear what happened:

ὁ ἀνεμος ἐστι μεγιστος. ὁ ἀνεμος φερει τας
ναυς προς την των Λωτοφαγων χωραν.
οἱ ἀνθρωποι τρεχουσι δια της χωρας.

Words

δια της χωρας = through the country
ὁ ἀνεμος = the wind
μεγιστος = very big
την των Λωτοφαγων χωραν = the land of the
Lotus Eaters

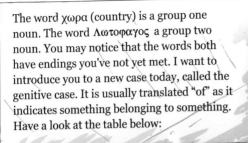

The word χωρα (country) is a group one noun. The word Λωτοφαγος a group two noun. You may notice that the words both have endings you've not yet met. I want to introduce you to a new case today, called the genitive case. It is usually translated "of" as it indicates something belonging to something. Have a look at the table below:

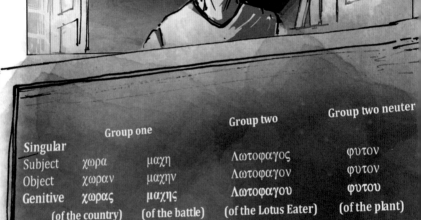

	Group one		Group two	Group two neuter
Singular				
Subject	χωρα	μαχη	Λωτοφαγος	φυτον
Object	χωραν	μαχην	Λωτοφαγον	φυτον
Genitive	χωρας	μαχης	Λωτοφαγου	φυτου
	(of the country)	(of the battle)	(of the Lotus Eater)	(of the plant)
Plural				
Subject	χωραι	μαχαι	Λωτοφαγοι	φυτα
Object	χωρας	μαχαι	Λωτοφαγους	φυτα
Genitive	χωρων	μαχων	Λωτοφαγων	φυτων
	(of the countries)	(of the battles)	(of the Lotus Eaters)	(of the plants)

The genitive also follows certain prepositions (words like "through" and "out of"). So δια της χωρας means "through the country". You may have noticed that the genitive singular ending for group one nouns is the same as the object plural. This may seem confusing, but you can usually tell which it is from the rest of the sentence.

You can look out for more genitive endings in the next few parts of my story.

οἱ ἄνθρωποι εὑρισκουσι τους Λωτοφαγους. οἱ Λωτοφαγοι ἐσθιουσι τον λωτον. ἐπει οἱ ἄνθρωποι ἐσθιουσι   τον λωτον, οὐκ ἐθελουσι ἐκβαινειν ἐκ της χωρας. οἱ ἄνθρωποι ἐθελουσι μενειν ἀει.

Words

ἀει = forever
ἐκ των νεων = from the ships
ἐκβαινειν = to go out
ἐπει = when
ἐσθιω = I eat
εὑρισκω = I find
ὁ λωτος = the lotus flower
μενειν = to stay

When my men had eaten the lotus plant, they forgot all about their lives beyond that land, and they just wanted to stay and eat the lotus, and never leave again.

It put them into a state of blissful forgetfulness, and I had to come and drag them away and back to the ship. They begged and begged to stay but I wouldn't let them back off the ship.

οἱ ἀνθρωποι ἐθελουσι ἐκβαινειν ἐκ των νεων και ἐσθιειν τον λωτον. λειπομεν την χωραν ἐν ταις ναυσι. οἱ ἀνθρωποι πασχουσι, ἀλλα χρη βαινειν.

Words

βαινειν = to go
λειπω = I leave
πασχω = I suffer
χρη = it is necessary

It was hard to see my men so unhappy, but if we had any hope of getting home, we had to get off that island and sail away. They longed for another taste of the plant that took all their worries away. After all we had been through, it's not a surprise that we all needed some comfort, but we had to move on. Little did we know quite how many adventures lay ahead of us.

Further Thoughts

There are lots of different plants called 'lotus' plants. Can you investigate them? Which one do you think might be the one my men ate? Or was it none of the ones you've discovered? Perhaps it was an entirely unknown plant. If so, what might it have looked and tasted like? Draw a picture or describe its texture and taste!

The lotus isn't the only plant to appear in the stories of my people. Here are few more Greek names of plants that are parts of stories you may have heard of. Can you transliterate them, and perhaps explore what plant they might be?

δαφνη   ἀνεμονη

ἀμυγδαλος   ἀσφοδελος

You'll find out about another plant, that rescued me from a dire fate, later in this book!

chapter 7

Polyphemus

So we got away from the Lotus Eaters with all our lives. The same cannot be said of our encounter with Polyphemus... We reached the island of the Cyclopes late one evening. The Cyclopes were one-eyed man-eating giants, so things were not likely to go well, although we didn't realise it then. Tired and longing for dry land and food, we left the ships and set up camp for the night. We ate what provisions we had and fell asleep almost straightaway.

The next morning, we started to look around and wonder who lived in this place. The island was wild and overgrown, and there was no sign of houses at all. We went to investigate.

εὑρίσκομεν ἀντρον. ἐν τῳ ἀντρῳ ἐστι τυρος. οὐκ ἐθελω ἐσθιειν τον τυρον, ἀλλα ἐμοι ἀνθρωποι ἐθελουσι ἐσθιειν τον τυρον. τελος, ἐσθιομεν τον τυρον.

Words
ἀντρον, το = cave
ἐμοι = my
τελος = finally
τυρος, ὁ = cheese

I'm sure you can the spot the problem here. If there is cheese in a cave, then the cave probably belongs to someone. In this case, it most definitely did belong to someone...

ἐστι το του Πολυφημου ἀντρον.

Before we go any further, I want to show you something funny that Greek does. Have a go at translating the sentence above into English. Odd, isn't it? This is one of the ways Greek has of expressing the genitive case. It gets called the genitive sandwich.

The sentence means "it is the cave of Polyphemus". The "of Polyphemus" is sandwiched between "the" and "cave". You can tell that the "το" goes with "ἀντρον", because "το" is the form of the definite article for neuter words, like ἀντρον.

Here are some other genitive sandwiches. Can you translate them?

ὁ του ἀνθρωπου βιβλος   βιβλος, ὁ = book

ἡ της θεας τιμη

Lets move on with the story...

νυκτι, ὁ Πολυφημος βαινει εἰς το ἀντρον. εὑρισκει ἐμους ἀνθρωπους. ἐσθιει δυο ἀνθρωπους. ἐξ ἡμερας βαινει ἐκ του ἀντρου.

Words

εἰς = into   ἐξ ἡμερας = by day

ἐκ = out of   νυκτι = in the night

I soon realised that I needed a plan to get us all out of that cave, before he munched his way through all my men. When he left in the morning with his sheep, he rolled a giant stone in front of the entrance, so we had no way of escaping. Except one...

When he returned that evening, I decided to have a chat with him.

"χαιρε, ὡ Πολυφημε" λεγω. "εἰμι Οὑτις και ἐχω δωρον. ἐχω οἰνον." ὁ Πολυφημος λαμβανει και πινει τον οἰνον.

Words

δωρον, το = gift

εἰμι = I am

ἐχω = I have

οἰνος, ὁ = wine

Οὑτις = No one

πινω = I drink

χαιρε = hello

ὡ = O

ὡ Πολυφημε = O Polyphemus

55

The Cyclops began to grow sleepy, while we sat and watched from the corner of the dark cave. At last his large eye drooped closed. We hoisted up a huge wooden rod and heated it on the dying embers of the fire. Then, when it was roasting hot, we plunged it deep into the socket of his eye!

ὁ τοῦ Πολυφήμου ὀφθαλμος σιζει.

σιζω = I sizzle, hiss

It was a loud crackling hiss, just as when someone puts a piece of hot metal into cold water. The Cyclops let out a huge howl.

The next morning, he rolled the stone away to let his sheep out. Little did he realise that we were clinging to the underside of his beloved sheep. That way, we made our escape!

Further Thoughts

That's not quite the end of that particular story. There is a reason I told Polyphemus that my name was "No one". When the Cyclops called out to the other cyclopes on his island, he declared "No one has blinded me!

Please help!

Of course, they thought he was quite mad, and thought it best to stay well away, which meant my men and I had a clear path to the seashore, and could climb aboard or ship and sail away.

I was very proud of my clever idea, although it got me into a bit of a scrape when I could not resist taunting the Cyclops as we sailed away. The Cyclopes are creatures which have intrigued artists and writers for centuries. There are so many different ways they have been imagined.

Draw your own version of the Cyclops, and decide whether you think he should look fierce, stupid, or even gentle. All of these have been created by artists.

There are those who think that maybe the story of the Cyclops came about because of these giant skulls of ancient animals with horns in the centre of their faces. Can you imagine a legendary creature that might come from a skeleton or skull of a different creature? Maybe even a person's skeleton or skull!

chapter 8

Circe

We escaped the dreadful island of Cyclopes, but we had lost some dear friends while there. We all sailed away feeling sad, though relieved to be still alive and back on our journey across the wine-dark sea.

As so often happened on this journey, we dodged one disaster to run headlong into another, and we encountered the god of the winds, Aeolus, and some fearful giants called the Laestrygonians.

I'll tell you about that another time, but for now, I will tell you what happened when our ship arrived on the island of the powerful sorceress, Circe.

ἡ Κιρκη ἐστι φαρμακις. ἐστι ἡ του Ἡλιου θυγατηρ.

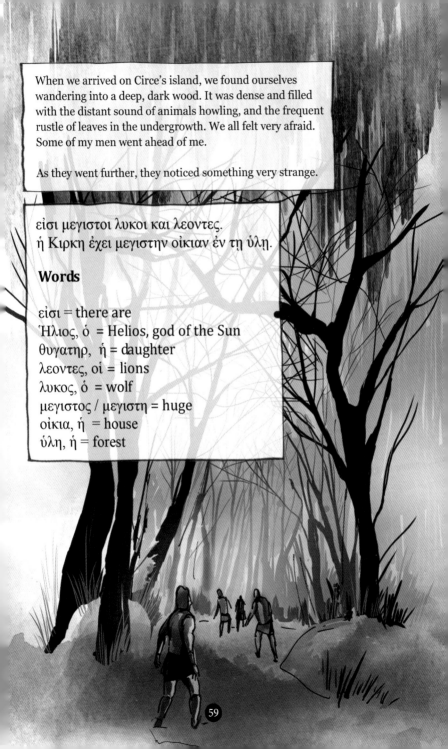

When we arrived on Circe's island, we found ourselves wandering into a deep, dark wood. It was dense and filled with the distant sound of animals howling, and the frequent rustle of leaves in the undergrowth. We all felt very afraid. Some of my men went ahead of me.

As they went further, they noticed something very strange.

εἰσι μεγιστοι λυκοι και λεοντες.
ἡ Κιρκη ἐχει μεγιστην οἰκιαν ἐν τῃ ὑλῃ.

Words

εἰσι = there are
Ἡλιος, ὁ = Helios, god of the Sun
θυγατηρ, ἡ = daughter
λεοντες, οἱ = lions
λυκος, ὁ = wolf
μεγιστος / μεγιστη = huge
οἰκια, ἡ = house
ὑλη, ἡ = forest

In Greek, as in many other languages, adjectives agree with the thing they are describing in gender and in number. So if the noun is the subject and is masculine and plural, then the ending of the adjective will change to agree with that, as with "μεγιστοι λυκοι".

In the case of the word "οἰκιαν", which is an object in its sentence, it also changed to agree (although with different letter, since group one nouns sometimes have an "α" and sometimes an "η").

Below are the adjective endings for adjectives like "μεγιστος":

Singular

	(feminine)	(masculine)	(neuter)
subject:	μεγιστη	μεγιστος	μεγιστον
object:	μεγιστην	μεγιστον	μεγιστον
genitive:	μεγιστης	μεγιστου	μεγιστου

Plural

	(feminine)	(masculine)	(neuter)
subject:	μεγισται	μεγιστοι	μεγιστα
object:	μεγιστας	μεγιστους	μεγιστα
genitive:	μεγιστων	μεγιστων	μεγιστων

Did you notice how the word "μεγιστος" changed depending on what it was describing?

Here are some other adjectives like "μεγιστος":

άγαθος, η, ον = good
δεινος, η, ον = terrible, strange
κακος, η, ον = bad
καλος, η, ον = beautiful
χαλεπος, η, ον = difficult

Can you translate the following phrases?

οἱ ἀγαθοι ἀνθρωποι
των δεινων θεων
καλη οἰκια

There they were, outside Circe's large house, with wolves and lions and other animals curled up sleepily on the ground or pacing back and forth. None of them seemed aggressive. They all seemed subdued and lost, so after a while, the men stopped being afraid that they might be attacked.

ἡ φαρμακις Κιρκη βαινει ἐκ της οἰκιας.
ἡ Κιρκη χαιρει ἐμους ἀνθρωπους.
βαινουσι εἰς την οἰκιαν. ἐν καλη τραπεζᾳ,
εἰσι τυροι, μελι και οἰνος.
ἐμοι ἀνθρωποι ἐσθιουσι και πινουσιν.
εὐθυς, εἰσι συες.

Words

ἐμους = my
εὐθυς = immediately
μελι = honey
τραπεζα, ἡ = table
συες = pigs

The sorceress Circe was very powerful, and her house was full of potions and herbs of all kinds which she had collected from the forest. She had mixed something in with the food and wine which had turned my men into pigs!

Luckily, one of my men had been suspicious and had run away without touching any of the food and drink. He came to tell me what had happened. Immediately, I rushed through the woods to rescue my men.

βαινω δια της ὑλης.
ὁ θεος Ἑρμης ἐστι ἐν τῃ ὑλῃ.
ὁ Ἑρμης παρεχει φυτον, μωλυ.

μωλυ = "moly"
φυτον, το = plant

I did not know what this
magical herb, moly,
would do, but I trusted
the god, ate the herb...

...and made my way through the wood to the palace of the sorceress
Circe, hoping to rescue my men and to save myself...

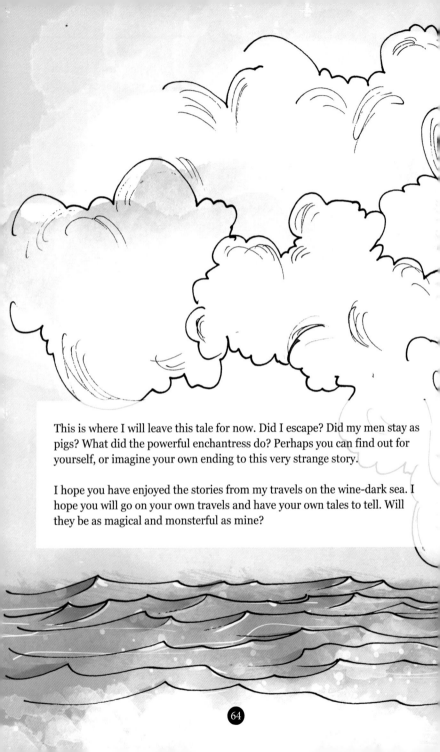

This is where I will leave this tale for now. Did I escape? Did my men stay as pigs? What did the powerful enchantress do? Perhaps you can find out for yourself, or imagine your own ending to this very strange story.

I hope you have enjoyed the stories from my travels on the wine-dark sea. I hope you will go on your own travels and have your own tales to tell. Will they be as magical and monsterful as mine?

Vocabulary

ἀγαθος, η, ον = good
ἀγω = I lead
ἀει = forever
ἀθλον, το = prize
ἀλλα = but
ἀνεμος, ὁ = wind
ἀντρον, το = cave
ἀποθνησκω = I die
ἀποκτεινω = I kill

βαινω = I go
βιβλος, ὁ = book

γυναικες, αἱ = women
γυνη, ἡ = woman

δεινος, η, ον = terrible, strange
δελφις, ἡ = dolphin
δημος, ὁ = the people
διοτι = because
δολος, ὁ = trick
δουλος, ὁ = a slave
δυοκαιδεκα = twelve
δωρον, το = gift

ἐθελω = I want
εἰ = you are
εἰμι = I am
εἰσι = they are
ἐχω = I have
εἰς = into/onto
ἐμος, η, ον = my
ἐν = in/on

ἑκατον = a hundred
ἐκβαινειν = to go out
ἑξηκοντα = sixty
ἐπει = when
ἐσθιω = I eat
εὐθυς = immediately
εὑρισκω = I find
ἐχω = I have

θεα, ἡ = goddess
θεος, ὁ = god
θυγατηρ, ἡ = daughter

ἱππος, ὁ = horse

και = and
κακος, η, ον = bad
καλλιστος, η, ον = very beautiful, the most beautiful
καλος, η, ον = beautiful

κορη, ἡ = girl
κυματωγη, ἡ = seashore

λαμβανω = I take
λεγω = I say
λειπω = I leave
λεοντες, οἱ = lions
λυκος, ὁ = wolf
λυρα, ἡ = lyre
λωτος, ὁ = the lotus flower

μαχη, ἡ = battle
μεγιστος, η, ον = very big, the biggest
μελι = honey
μενω = I stay
μηλον, το = apple

ναυς, ἡ = ship
νοσος, ἡ = disease
νυν = now

ὀγδοηκοντα = eighty
ὁδος, ἡ = road
οἰκια, ἡ = house
οἰνος, ὁ = wine
ὀμφαλος, ὁ = omphalos stone (navel)
ὁπλα, τα = weapons
ὀργη, ἡ = anger

πασχω = I suffer
πεμπω = I send
πεντηκοντα = fifty
πινω = I drink
πολεμιοι, οἱ = the enemy
πολυμητις = wily, clever
πολις, ἡ = city
πολλοι = many
προς = towards
πυλη, ἡ = gate

σιζω = I sizzle, hiss
σοφια, ἡ = wisdom
στρατος, ὁ = army
συες = pigs

τελος = finally
τιμη, ἡ = honour
τοξον, το = bow
τραπεζα, ἡ = table
τρεχω = I run
τυρος, ὁ = cheese

ὑλη, ἡ = forest

φιλος, ὁ = friend
φυτον, το = plant

χαιρε = hello
χαλεπος, η, ον = difficult
χρη = it is necessary
χρυσεος, η, ον = golden
χωρα, ἡ = country

ὠ = o

Afterword

I loved Greek myths and stories from a very young age, thanks largely to the *Usborne Greek Myths and Legends*, which my parents bought for me and my brother. I remember that it contained the most striking images and tales of strange creatures and vengeful gods. There was something unearthly and powerful about them, something that drew me in, and made me want to stay in that world to explore further. A ghostly Cerberus, a huge minotaur with twisting horns, the faces of gods and heroes, all these looked out at me from those pages and lured me inside.

I continued to read and experience the Greek myths in many forms as I grew up; this included the inimitable *Ulysses 31*, a futuristic take on the stories of Odysseus which my brother and I used to rush home to see after school! It was not until I was sixteen or seventeen, though, that I first encountered Homer's *Iliad*. There we were, sitting in a chilly classroom one autumn morning, reading book six of the *Iliad*, as our teacher introduced us to the simile of the generations of men being like leaves, which the wind scatters across the land. We were teenagers in the mid-nineties, reading words that would have been heard thousands of years ago, and feeling the same sense of fragile and fleeting mortality. It wasn't just the meaning of those words that struck a deep chord within me, but how the meaning was entwined with the flow of the poetry (those words are now written large on the wall of my small office at school, and many students who comes to see me in here comment on them).

I had never read anything like it. I had read poetry and prose before, but nothing with such lyrical beauty. Soon, I discovered more of the beauty of the words. Refrains describing things like the glistening sea, the gleaming lights of many camp fires, the rosy glow of dawn, all expressed with the mesmerising rhythm of a song. I remember loving the rich detail of the language, which provided unexpected windows into daily life from so long ago: children clinging to their mothers' dresses, a baby startled by a hero's helmet, and women washing clothes in the springs, flies buzzing round a milk pail. It was a feast of the senses, and the experience swept me along.

When I began to read the *Odyssey*, I enjoyed this same detail and style. I remember the hiss of the metal as it plunged into the Cyclops' eye, which I felt I had to incorporate into this book!

Unlike the *Iliad*, the *Odyssey* is brimming with magic. The ghastly Cyclops and the sinister Circe, with her knowledge of herbs and roots, are archetypal fairy tale creatures. The Lotus Eaters, too, in their hazy land of forgetfulness, Aeolus, with his bag of winds, and even the Phaeacians with their swift ships, all recall the sort of magical beings and mysterious artefacts that inhabit the folktale universe. They were very different stories from the ones I knew in the *Iliad*. There, the world was filled with the grim realities of war and blood, interspersed with the daily lives of ordinary humans, in a way that was profoundly moving to me. The world of the *Odyssey* was filled with adventure, mystery, magic and wonder. It had a very different atmosphere, at once less serious, but more magical.

It also possesses the voice of Odysseus himself, telling these magical stories, always leaving us with the question of what actually happened, and what he has embellished or invented. Was he really the brave leader of his men he appeared to be, or was there more to be said about the fact that he lost every last one of them before he reached his beloved Ithaca?

I hope that this book captures a little of the wonder of both the *Iliad* and the *Odyssey*. The stories, with the vivid illustrations by Soham De, are chosen because they are parts of the two epics which particularly stand out to me: the fierce, hot-headed argument on the beach between the two heroes, who later run around the city walls, Achilles chasing after doomed Hector; the clever and devastating trick of the wooden horse, the Lotus Eaters, Cyclops and Circe.

Of course, there are many more wonderful stories which I have not included in these chapters. The aim was never to create a comprehensive retelling!

Unlike *Telling Tales in Latin*, its counterpart in Greek requires the introduction of an entirely new alphabet, and so I decided I would sprinkle Greek words through the first chapter in order to build up practice of recognising and pronouncing the new letters. Throughout the book, much of the story is told in English text, as well, since the introduction of the Greek is far slower.

As mentioned in my acknowledgements, I trialled this book on a group of students I run a Greek GCSE club for at Cheney School. One of these students, Barnaby Evans, has written his own piece on why the *Iliad* and the *Odyssey* are such appealing stories, and I have included this below as the final part of this afterword.

Lorna Robinson

The epics of Homer

The *Iliad* and the *Odyssey* will always inspire and intrigue. Even today, when black ships rarely amass to avenge the honour of kings and savage, one-eyed giants are firmly within the realms of myth, these stories continue to fascinate us. Perhaps it's our inherent love of the fantastical: that these legends are read over and over again simply because they are so different to our normal lives, because we love the excitement of bickering gods and heroes struggling towards their fate.

But Homer's work is so much more than that of a fantasist. Of course, his status as a single historic figure is disputed, but the works that have been ascribed to him lay down the foundations of the entirety of western literature. Without the *Iliad* and the *Odyssey*, there would have been no tradition for the *Aeneid* to draw on, no *Paradise Lost* to follow it, and so on. The entire landscape of arts would be completely different. This is in part why the stories of the *Iliad* and the *Odyssey* have never lost their appeal: by reading them we see the blueprint of all the other stories we know and love: the original archetypes from which the greatest books are based.

This timelessness though is not simply due to the vast influence the *Iliad* and the *Odyssey* have had over western culture, but also in the issues and themes these works deal with. The *Iliad* is a work, primarily, concerning the wrath of Achilles, and such issues of struggling with emotions, following one's fate or purpose, and the limits of our virtues, cut right to the very of core of the human condition and makes these works eternally relatable. The *Odyssey* too, with its myriad of peoples and monsters scattered across the Mediterranean that begins to point to what is common between all people, and what it truly is to be civilized. This technique of presenting other cultures to highlight one's own, later adopted from Homer by Swift in *Gulliver's Travels*, makes us question our perception of humanity and civilization, as relevant to our world now as it was when Homer wrote it. This, arguably, is why people hundreds of years from now will be able to read Homer's epics and still are just as moved as those who first read it.

Barnaby Evans, Greek GCSE student at Cheney School

Available in ebook and in a paperback edition

"Really inviting and engaging, with clear explanations and beautiful and fun illustrations by Soham De . . . Excellent for projects introducing . . . An inviting, absorbing and embracing learning experience." The Classics Library

Telling Tales in Latin

Lorna Robinson
Illustrated by Soham De

Ovid's *Metamorphoses*, stories that explore many of the founding myths of Western literature, have been popular literature for millennia. In *Telling Tales in Latin* they are the perfect resource for teaching Latin and general literacy skills.

Each chapter introduces one of Ovid's much-loved stories, encouraging children to begin reading Latin immediately while exploring the literary and mythic context of the stories. At the end of each chapter there are suggested activities to help learners to think about what they have just read. From Daedalus to the story of Orpheus, Lorna Robinson uses Ovid's stories to teach Latin grammar and vocabulary, exploring the relationship between Latin and English grammar to enhance the child's literacy as well as encouraging children's imaginations by asking them to discuss how Ovid's themes are still topical today.

Telling Tales in Latin has been specially designed to incorporate all the vocabulary and grammar needed for OCR entry level Latin, Lorna Robinson also provides an ideal introduction to the inspirational nature of Roman culture, literature, philosophy and history.

"Combines mythical storytelling with an introduction to Latin, building grammar and vocabulary." The School Run

Distant Lands:
Telling Tales in Latin 2

Lorna Robinson
Illustrated by Soham De

Distant Lands is a companion volume to Lorna Robinson's
Telling Tales in Latin. Also narrated by the poet Ovid who tells the tale of his own exile, along with more well-loved tales from *Metamorphoses*.

Introducing readers to the history of Ovid's life and exile, as well as learning about the geography of the Roman Empire, **Distant Lands** will engage pupils in stories such as Lycaon, the wild man who became a wolf, and Pyramus and Thisbe, the love-struck pair who whisper through a crack in their adjoining wall. These stories are woven into Ovid's account of his last night in Rome, his dramatic journey across the seas, and the strangeness of the new world that he discovers.

Soham De's illustrations bring Ovid's stories alive and make learning Latin an imaginative journey of discovery while Lorna Robinson outlines how Latin is the basis for English grammar, unlocking the complexities of learning English (and other languages) along the way. Each story is accompanied with creative activities that update the stories around contemporary issues from history, geography, philosophy and literature.